BOOK THREE

A DOZEN A DAY

Technical Exercises
FOR THE PIANO
to be done each day
BEFORE practicing

by

Edna Mae Burnam

Includes Online Audio Orchestrations by Ric Ianonne

PLAYBACK+
Speed • Pitch • Balance • Loop

The exclusive **PLAYBACK+** feature allows tempo changes without altering the pitch.
Loop points can also be set for repetition of tricky measures.

To access audio, visit:
www.halleonard.com/mylibrary

7808-3133-1080-0059

ISBN 978-1-4234-5292-8

WILLIS MUSIC

EXCLUSIVELY DISTRIBUTED BY

HAL•LEONARD®

7777 W. BLUEMOUND RD. P.O. BOX 13819
MILWAUKEE, WISCONSIN 53213

Visit Hal Leonard Online at
www.halleonard.com

To my good friend, Mr. Carl W. Yager

A DOZEN A DAY

Many people do exercises every morning before they go to work.

Likewise—we should give our fingers exercises every day before we begin our practicing.

The purpose of this book is to help develop strong hands and flexible fingers.

The finger exercises may be played slowly and softly at first; then gradually faster and louder.

The chord exercises may be played *mp*, *mf*, and *f* for variation, and at a moderate rate of speed.

Do not try to learn the entire first dozen exercises the first week you study this book! Just learn two or three exercises and do them each day *before* practicing. When these are mastered, add another, then another, and keep adding until the twelve can be played perfectly.

When the first dozen—or Group I—has been mastered and perfected, Group II may be introduced in the same manner, and so on for the other Groups.

Any of the Groups may be transposed to different Keys. In fact, this should be encouraged.

EDNA MAE BURNAM

INDEX

Group I

1. Off With The Covers and Out Of Bed!

*First time **mp** - warm water*
*Second time **f** - cold water*

2. In The Shower (shivering)

3. Indian Clubs

4. Walking On Rings

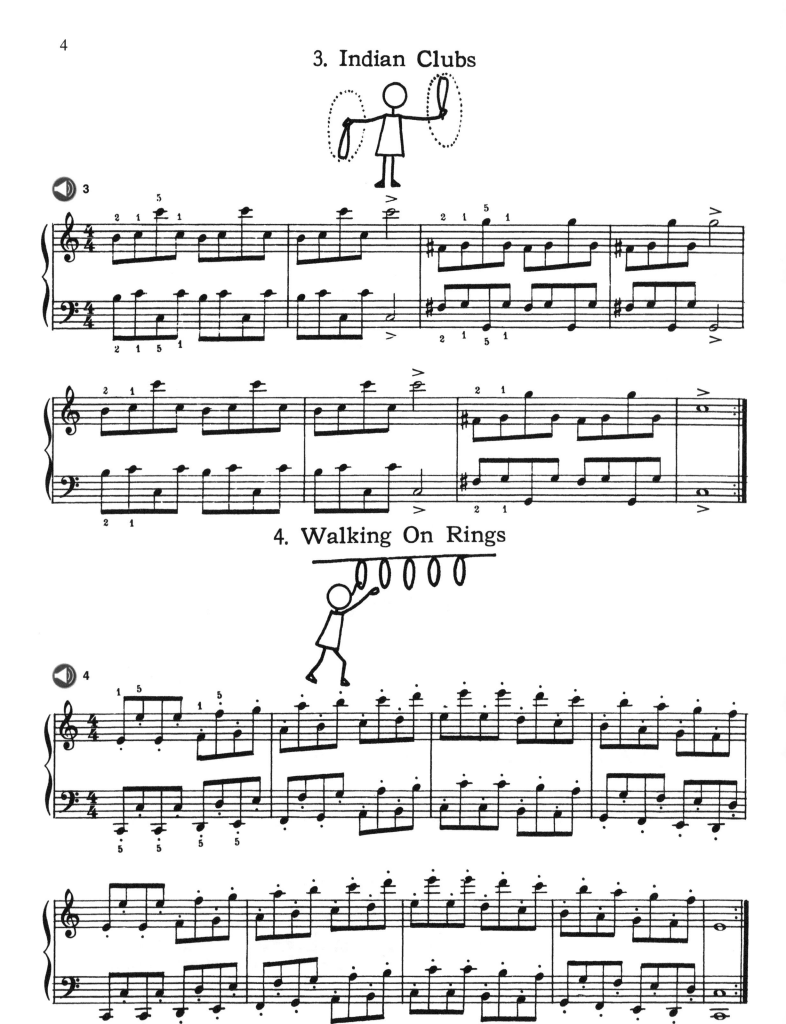

5. Climbing (in place)

6. Lariat Practice

7. Going Downstairs

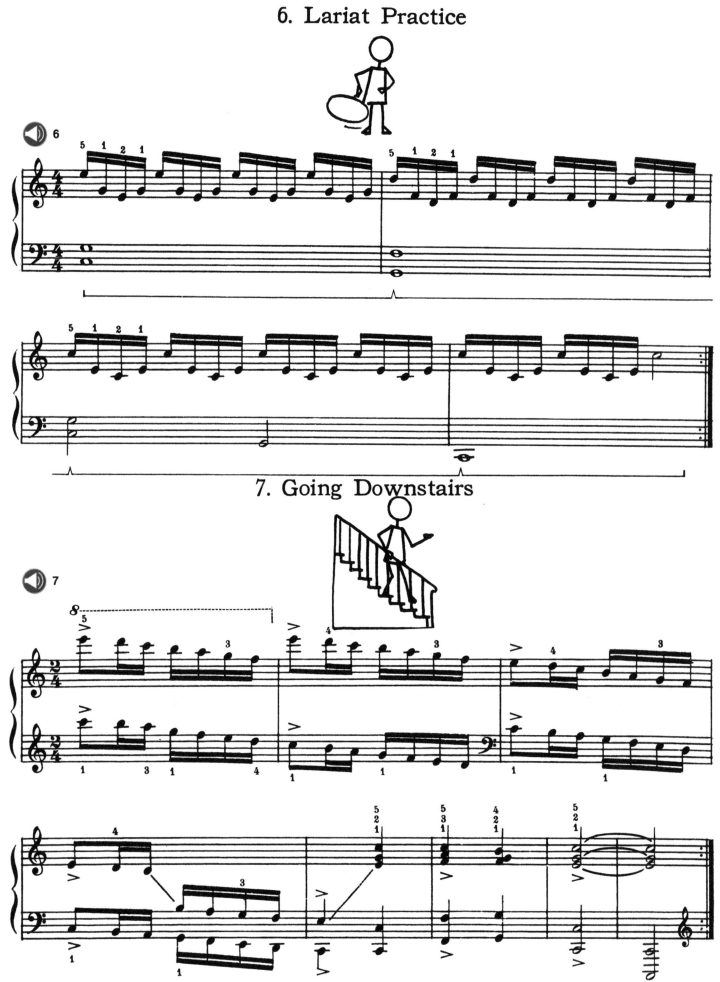

8. Whirling A Baton

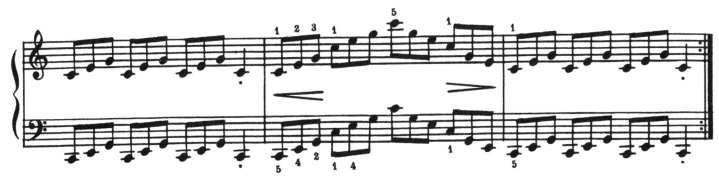

9. Punching Bag Exercise

10. Deep Breathing

11. Cartwheels

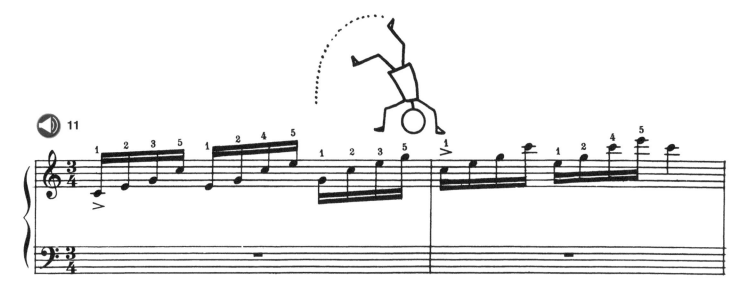

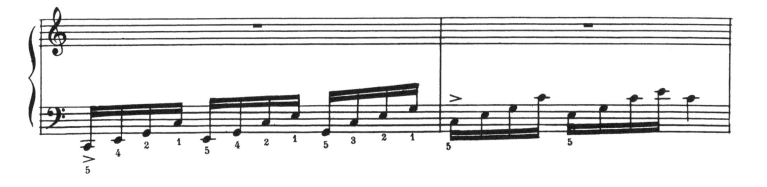

12. Fit As A Fiddle and Ready To Go

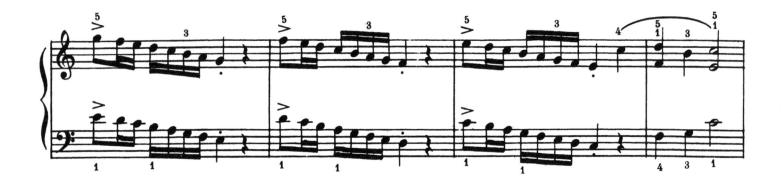

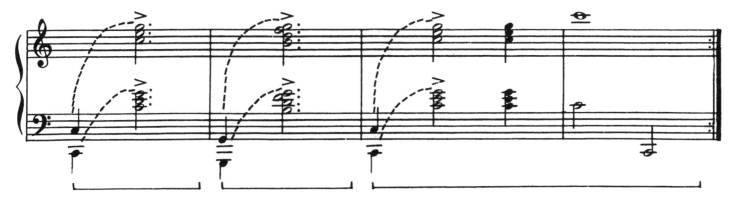

Group II

1. Deep Breathing

2. Jumping On A Gym Horse

3. Jumping Off A Gym Horse

4. Golf Practice

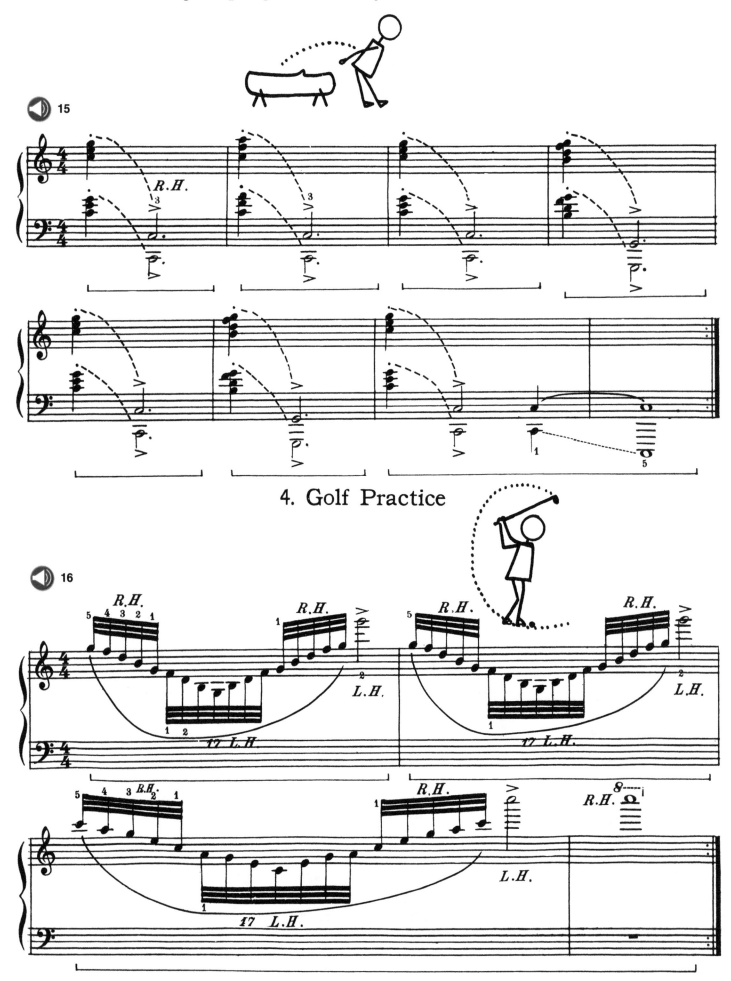

5. Weight Lifting

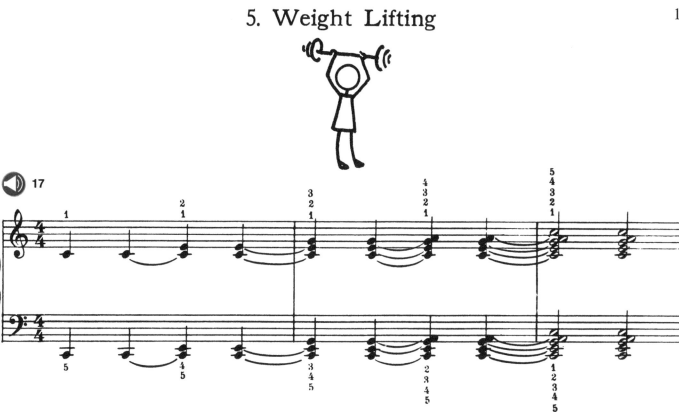

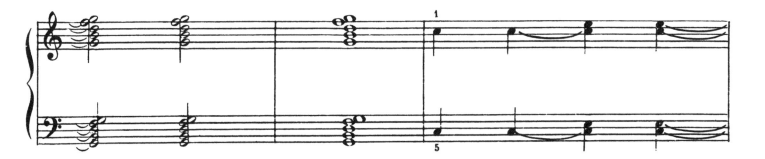

6. Pole Vaulting

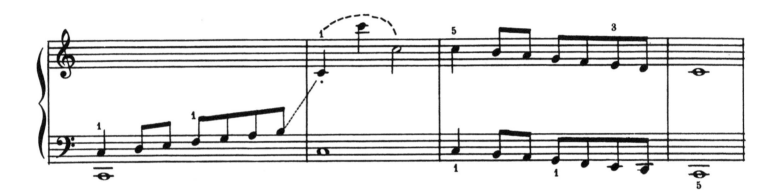

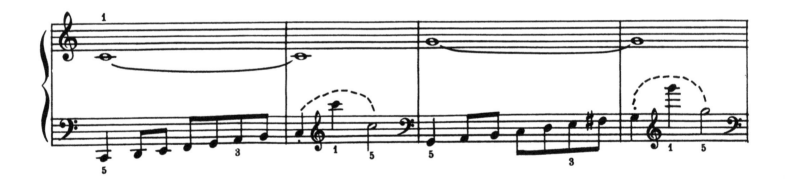

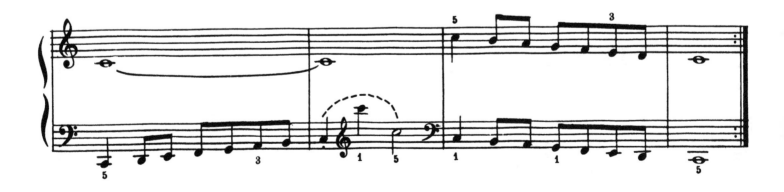

7. Climbing (in place)

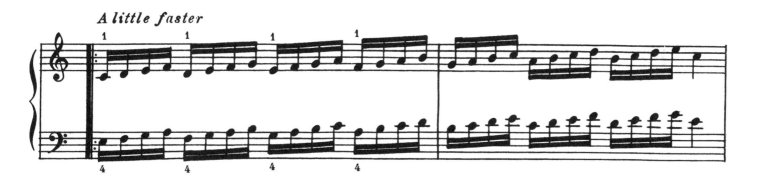

8. Jump Rope

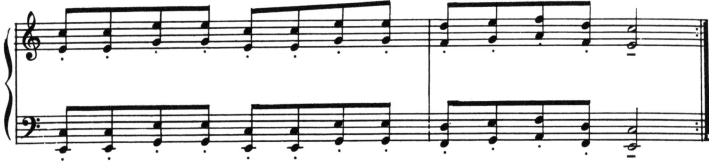

Red Pepper

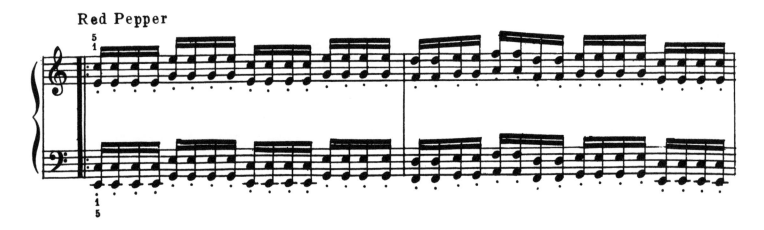

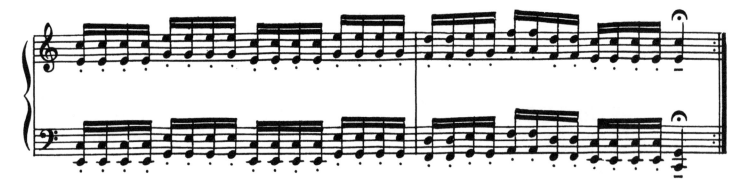

9. The Splits

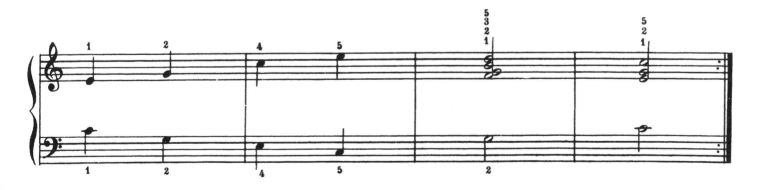

10. Going Upstairs and Downstairs

11. Cartwheels

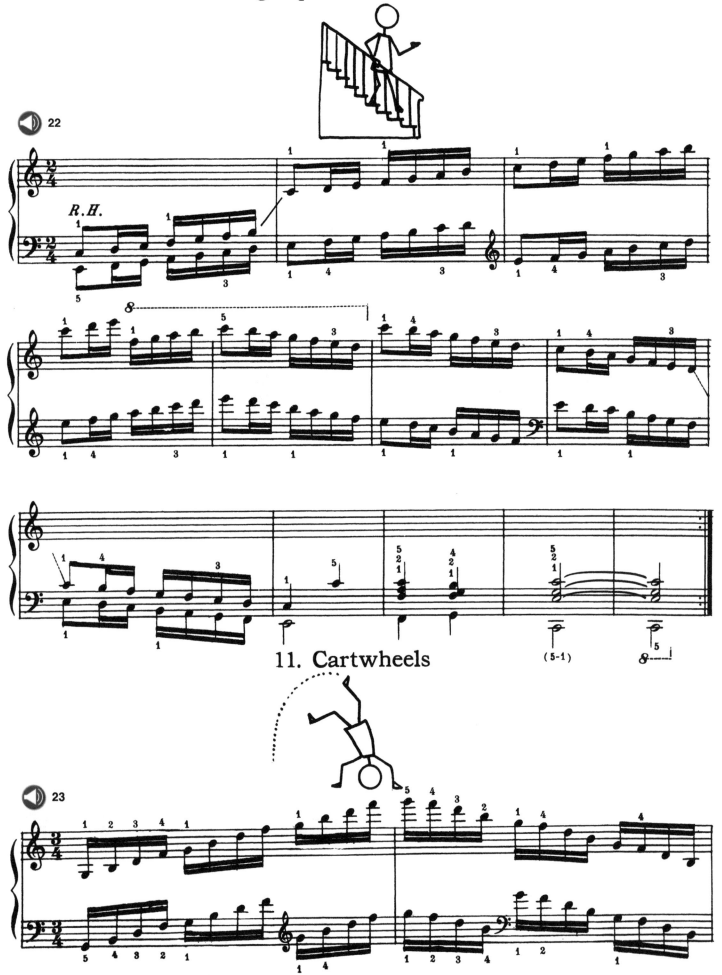

12. Fit As A Fiddle and Ready To Go

Group III
1. Basket Ball Practice

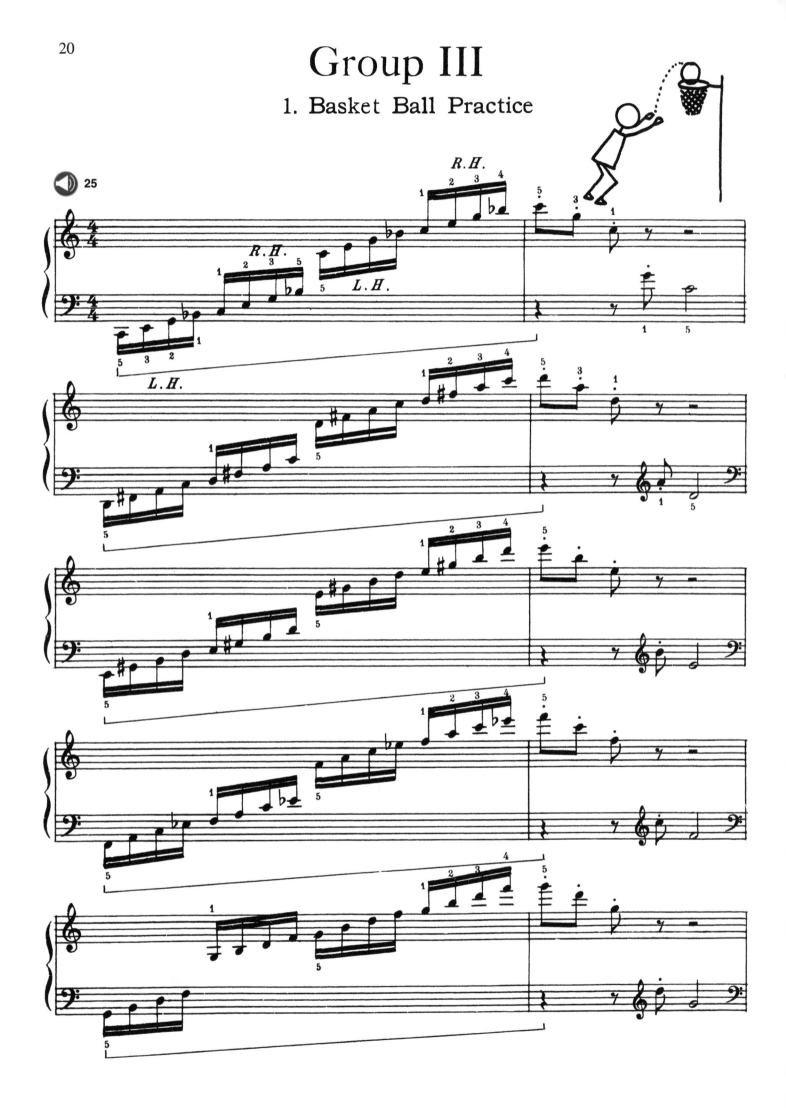

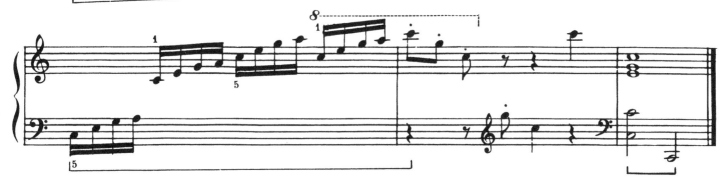

2. Rolling

3. French Jump Rope (two ropes)

4. Running

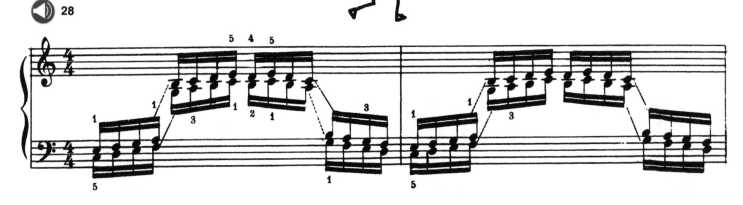

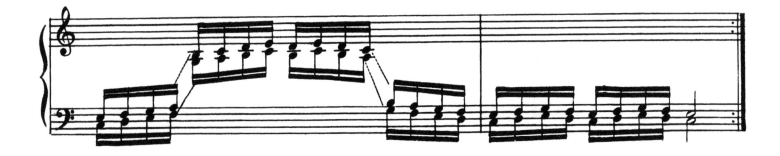

5. Baby Steps

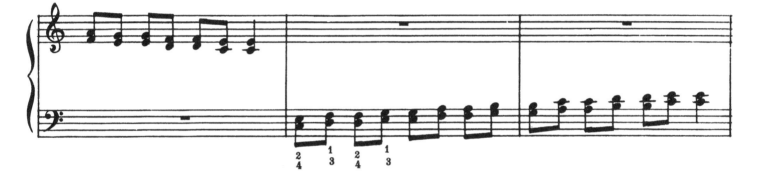

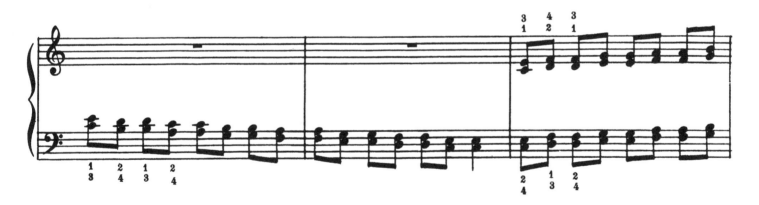

24

6. Daddy Longleg Steps

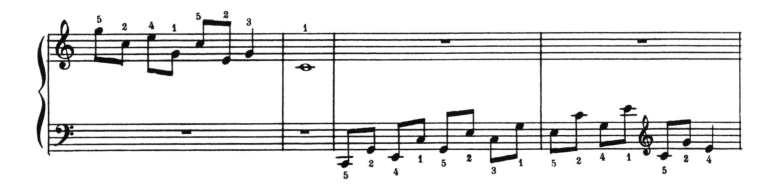

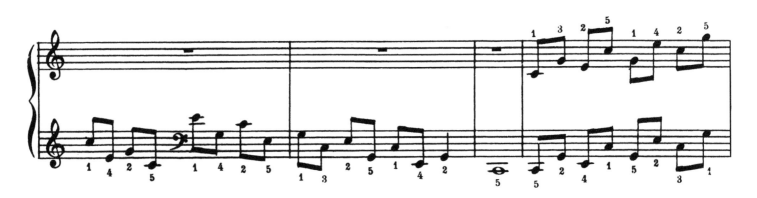

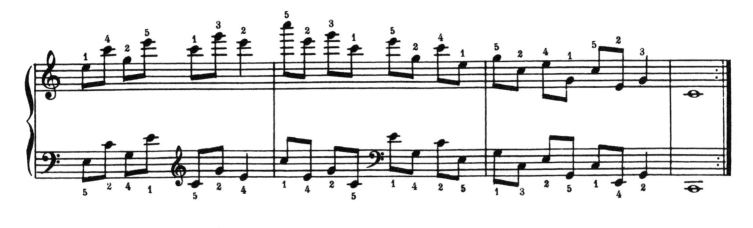

7. Rolling A Hoop

26

8. Deep Breathing

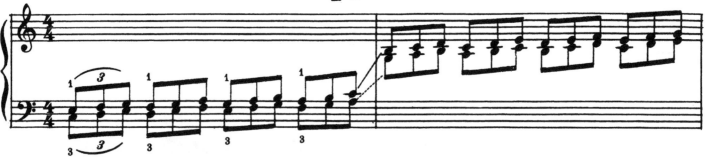

9. Climbing In Place

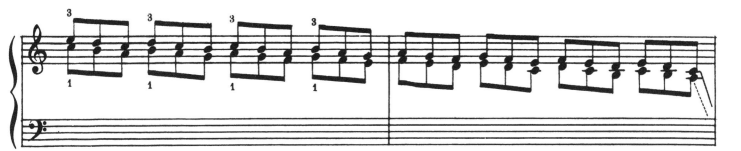

10. Going Upstairs and Downstairs

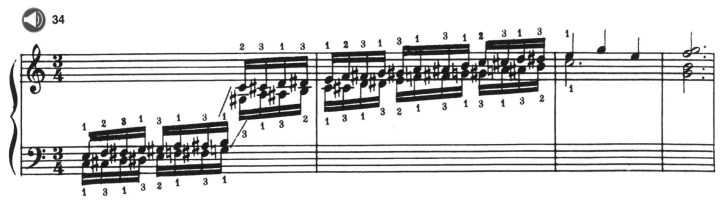

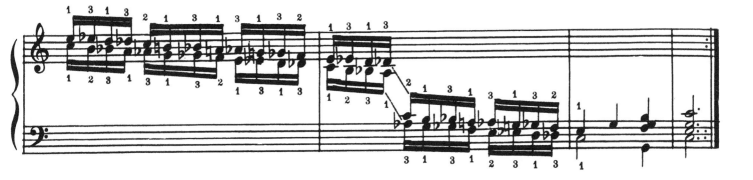

11. Reaching Up Very High

12. Fit As A Fiddle and Ready To Go

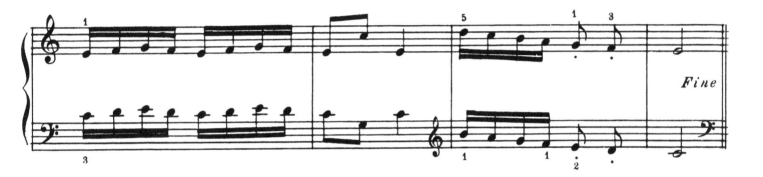

Group IV

1. Ping Pong

2. Flinging Arms Out and Back

3. Swimming Exercise (flutter kick)

4. Swimming Exercise (arm stroke)

5. Swimming Exercise (breathing)

41

Set fingers silent.
Hold down throughout two measures.

Putting face in water and out for a quick breath 8 times.

Set fingers silent.
Hold down throughout two measures.

Putting face in water and out for a quick breath 4 times.

Set fingers silent.
Hold down throughout two measures.

Putting face in water and out for a little bigger breath 4 times.

Set fingers silent.
Hold down throughout two measures.

Putting face in water and out and breathing evenly

6. Walking On Toes

7. Twirling On Toe

8. Deep Breathing

9. Cartwheels

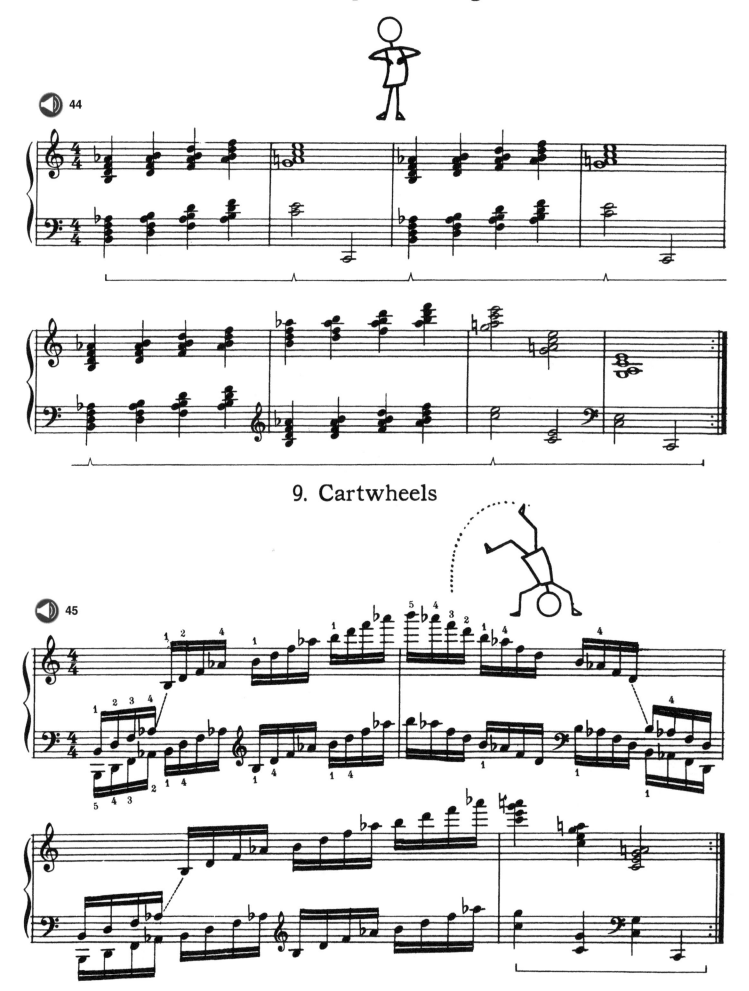

10. Upstairs and Downstairs

On a Cloudy Day

On a Sunny Day

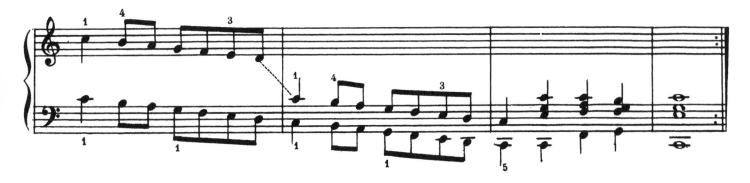

11. Bowling

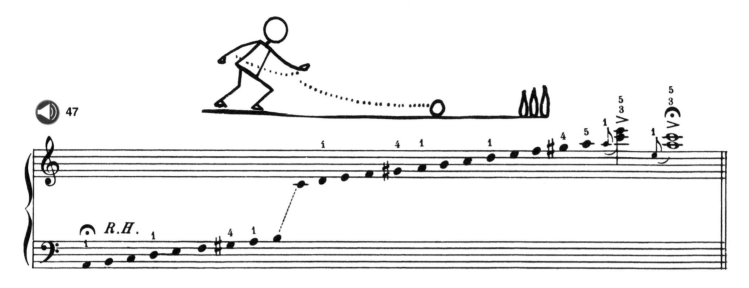

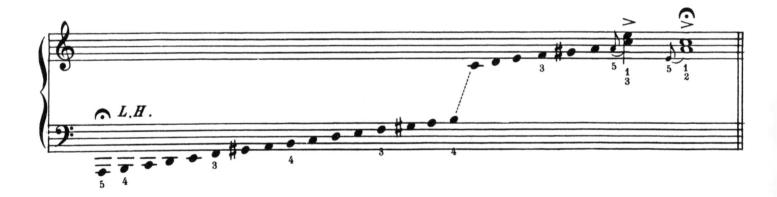

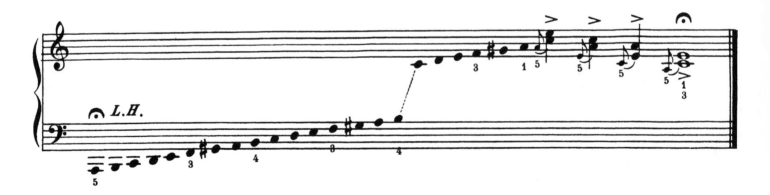

12. Fit As A Fiddle and Ready To Go

Group V

1. Deep Breathing

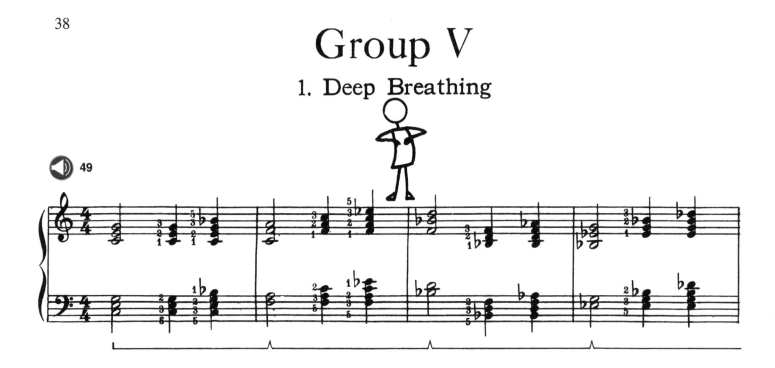

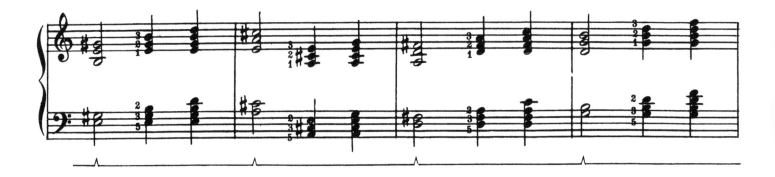

2. Jumping Hurdles "C" "E" and "G"
(Say names of hurdles aloud as you jump each one.)

3. Going Upstairs and Downstairs

two steps at a time

three steps at a time

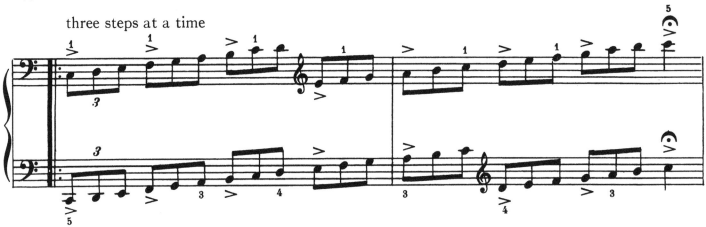

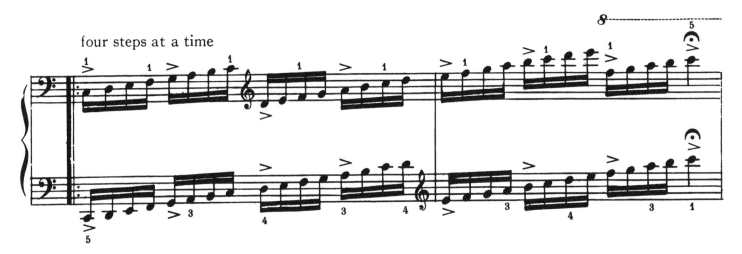

four steps at a time

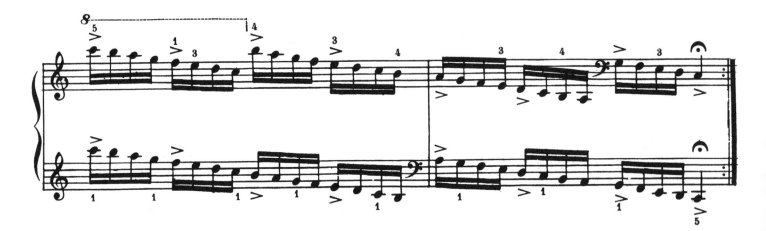

4. Walking On Stilts

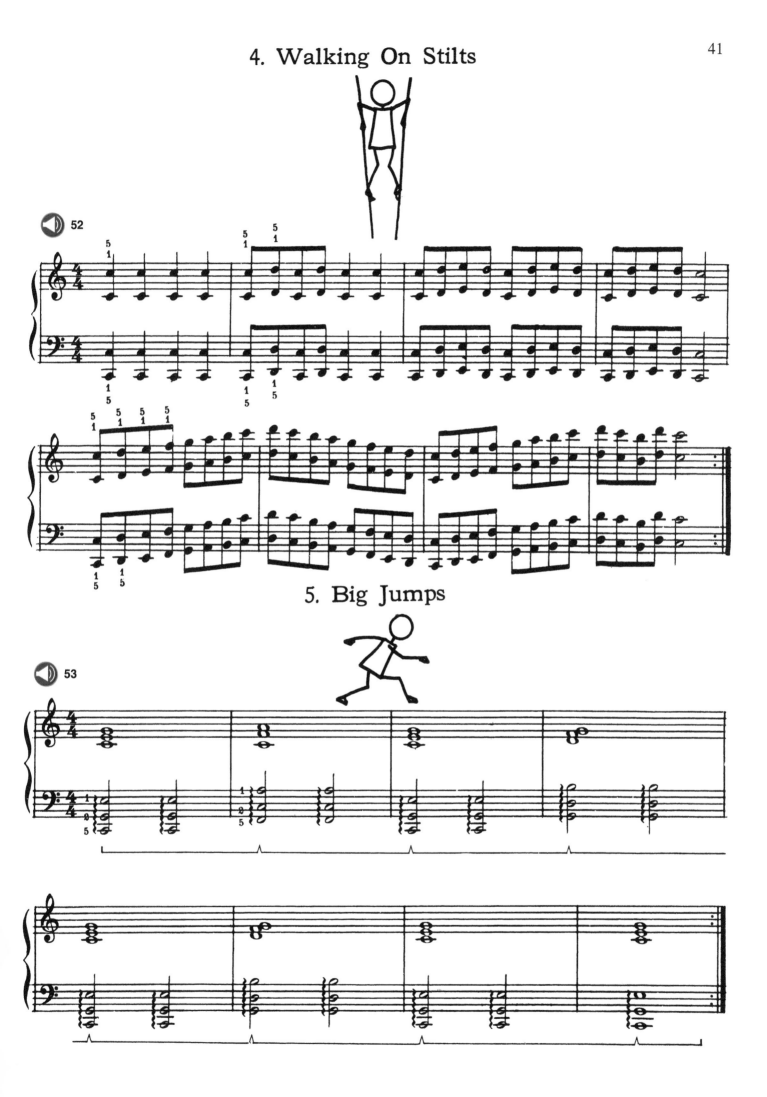

5. Big Jumps

6. Tether Ball

7. High Kicking

8. Follow The Leader

🔊 56

Left Hand leader
Right Hand follows

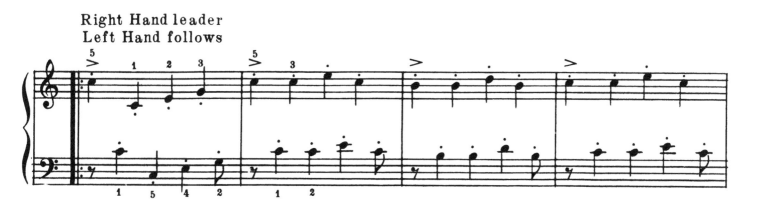

Right Hand leader
Left Hand follows

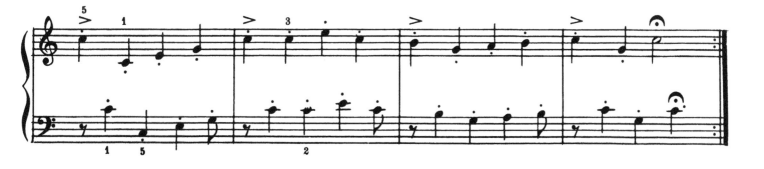

9. Tumbling

10. Swinging On Rings and Walking

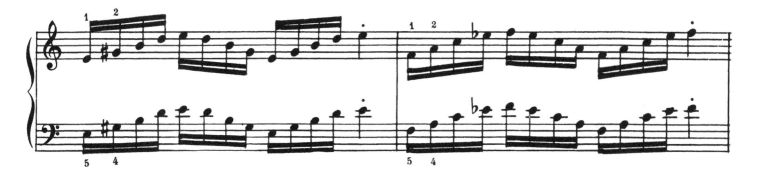

11. Water Skiing

12. Fit As A Fiddle and Ready To Go

A DOZEN A DAY

by Edna Mae Burnam

The **A Dozen A Day** books are universally recognized as one of the most remarkable technique series on the market for all ages! Each book in this series contains short warm-up exercises to be played at the beginning of each practice session, providing excellent day-to-day training for the student. All book/audio versions include orchestrated accompaniments by Ric Ianonne.

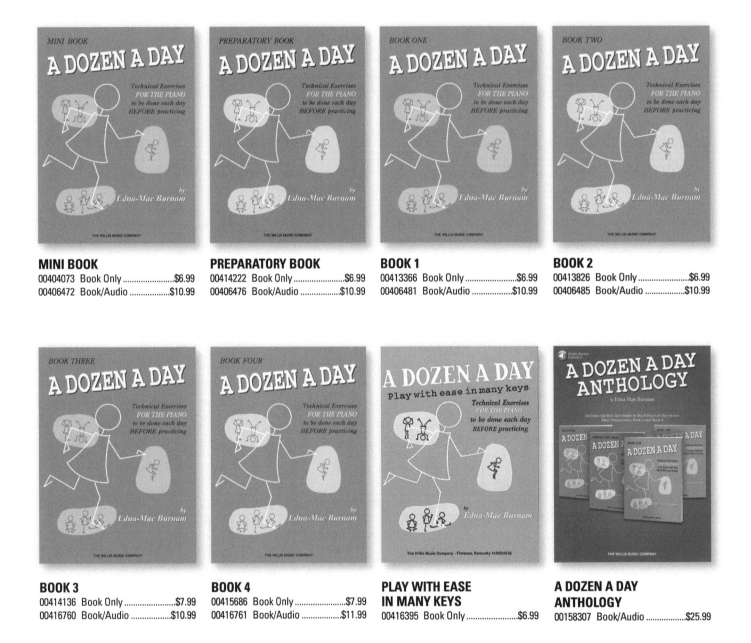

MINI BOOK
00404073 Book Only $6.99
00406472 Book/Audio $10.99

PREPARATORY BOOK
00414222 Book Only $6.99
00406476 Book/Audio $10.99

BOOK 1
00413366 Book Only $6.99
00406481 Book/Audio $10.99

BOOK 2
00413826 Book Only $6.99
00406485 Book/Audio $10.99

BOOK 3
00414136 Book Only $7.99
00416760 Book/Audio $10.99

BOOK 4
00415686 Book Only $7.99
00416761 Book/Audio $11.99

**PLAY WITH EASE
IN MANY KEYS**
00416395 Book Only $6.99

**A DOZEN A DAY
ANTHOLOGY**
00158307 Book/Audio $25.99

ALSO AVAILABLE:
The **A Dozen A Day Songbook** series containing Broadway, movie, and pop hits!

Visit Hal Leonard Online at www.halleonard.com

WILLIS MUSIC

EXCLUSIVELY DISTRIBUTED BY

HAL•LEONARD®

Prices, contents, and availability subject to change without notice. Prices listed in U.S. funds.